I am grateful to god for everything! And I believe that the meaning of life is to make sense of other lives. A.D.R., you are the meaning of my life.

全てにおいて神様に感謝しています！ そして、人生の意味とは他の人生の意味を理解することだと私は信じています。A.D.R.、あなたは私の人生の意味です。

Leandro Garcia

2024

L.G.P©
Leandro Garcia Publications

This book belongs to:＿＿＿＿＿＿＿
この本は*のものだ:

SAMURAI

Color test page:
カラーテストページ

Samurai
The story of the Samurai

Honor. Justice. Perfection. Loyalty.
These are some of the words associated with the Samurai, the warrior class of feudal Japan and to this day, their influence is felt in the way of living and thinking of the Japanese people.

The samurai emerged, as a warrior class, in feudal times in Japan and dominated the country for almost eight centuries (8th to 19th centuries). Being a samurai was a social prestige, since the warrior class occupied the highest positions within the Japanese military dictatorship, called the Shogunate or Bakufu.

Modern Samurai are people who, nowadays, apply BUSHIDO and practice the arts of the sword in the country for almost eight centuries (8th to 19th century). Being a samurai was a social prestige, since the warrior class occupied the highest positions within the Japanese military dictatorship, called the Shogunate or Bakufu.

Initially, the samurai's role was just to collect taxes and serve the Empire. From the 10th century onwards, the figure of the samurai took shape and gained a series of military functions, reaching its peak in the 17th century. The martial styles created by the Samurai today are called Kobudo (古武道). It was through the practice of these styles that the samurai perfected their techniques, strengthened their spirit and aimed for improvement, with self-discipline and self-control. But what made this warrior unique was his famous code of honor and conduct, Bushido. In addition to the philosophy assimilated by the samurai, Bushido brought precepts for correct behavior in all situations.

"He who serves"
Samurai (kanji: 侍) literally means "one who serves", a legacy from when they were directly subordinate to the emperor. Another term often used to refer to samurai is Bushi (武士), which literally means "warrior". It is the root of the word Bushido (武士道), or "Way of the Warrior".
Niten Institute BR

The Last Samurai

In 1868, with the Meiji Restoration, the samurai class was abolished and a Western-style national army was established. Even with these reforms, the samurai did not let their tradition die. The sword arts created in feudal times were cultivated and passed down from generation to generation until the present day. And Bushido survived in its purest form within Kobudo dojos.

Currently, the arts of ancient samurai are practiced with the aim of helping people overcome obstacles in their daily lives and acquire tranquility, control, discipline and self-confidence.

Modern Samurai are, therefore, people who apply the philosophy of Bushido today and practice the arts of the sword, keeping an 800-year-old tradition alive.

"Kobudo is made up of a large number of styles (in Japanese ryu), which are taught even in Japan, the opportunity to learn some styles of Kobudo is rare, the techniques of the different weapons used by Samurais, such as Kenjutsu (techniques with sword), Jojutsu (staff technique), Naginatajutsu (halberd), among many others." Niten Institute BR

武士

サムライの物語

名誉。 正義。 完璧。 忠誠心。
これらは封建時代の日本の武士階級である武士に関連した言葉の一部であり、今日に至るまで日本人の生き方や考え方にその影響が感じられています。

武士は日本の封建時代に戦士階級として出現し、ほぼ 8 世紀 (8 世紀から 19 世紀) にわたって日本を支配しました。 武士階級は、幕府または幕府と呼ばれる日本の軍事独裁政権内で最高の地位を占めていたため、武士であることは社会的威信でした。

現代の武士は、今日ではほぼ 8 世紀 (8 世紀から 19 世紀) にわたってこの国で武士道を実践し、剣術を練習してきた人々です。 武士階級は、幕府または幕府と呼ばれる日本の軍事独裁政権内で最高の地位を占めていたため、武士であることは社会的威信でした。

当初、武士の役割は税金を集めて帝国に奉仕することだけでした。 10世紀以降、武士の姿が形成され、一連の軍事的機能を獲得し、17世紀に最盛期に達しました。

今日の武士によって生み出された武道は古武道と呼ばれます。 武士はこの流儀の実践を通じて技を磨き、精神を鍛え、自制心と自制心を持って向上を目指しました。 しかし、この戦士をユニークなものにしたのは、彼の有名な名誉と行動規範である武士道でした。 武士道は、武士が吸収した哲学に加えて、あらゆる状況における正しい行動のための教訓をもたらしました。

「仕える者」

侍（漢字：侍）は文字通り「仕える者」を意味し、天皇に直属していた時代からの名残です。 武士を指すのによく使われるもう 1 つの用語は、文字通り「戦士」を意味する「武士」です。 それは武士道、または「戦士の道」という言葉の語源です。

ラストサムライ

1868年、明治維新により士族階級が廃止され、西洋式の国軍が創設された。こうした改革があっても、武士は伝統を絶やさなかった。封建時代に生み出された剣術は培われ、現代まで脈々と受け継がれてきました。そして武士道は古武道の道場の中で最も純粋な形で生き残ったのです。

現在、古代の武士の芸術は、人々が日常生活の障害を克服し、平静、制御、規律、自信を獲得するのを助けることを目的として実践されています。

したがって、現代の武士は、武士道の哲学を今日に応用し、800年の伝統を守りながら剣術を実践する人々です。

「古武道は、日本でも教えられている多数の流派で構成されていますが、古武道の一部の流派や、剣術などの武士が使用するさまざまな武器の技術を学ぶ機会は稀です。剣術）、杖術（杖術）、薙刀術（ハルバード）など。Niten Institute BR

JAPANESE ARCHITECTURE
HOUSES, SCENERY AND TEMPLES

日本建築
家と風景と寺院

Traditional houses are called Minka (民家), which literally means "people's house". The style originates from the Edo period and the appearance varies greatly from region to region. These residences have Japanese-style rooms called Washitsu (和室).

伝統的な家は民家（民家）と呼ばれ、文字通り「人々の家」を意味します。江戸時代に起源を持ち、地域によってその姿は大きく異なります。これらの住居には和室と呼ばれる和室があります。

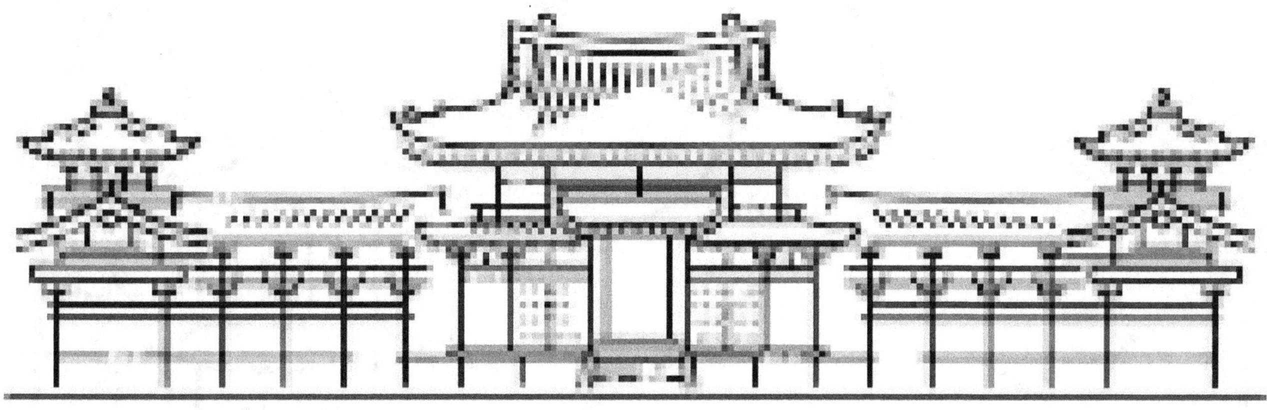

KYOTO

祈りの神殿

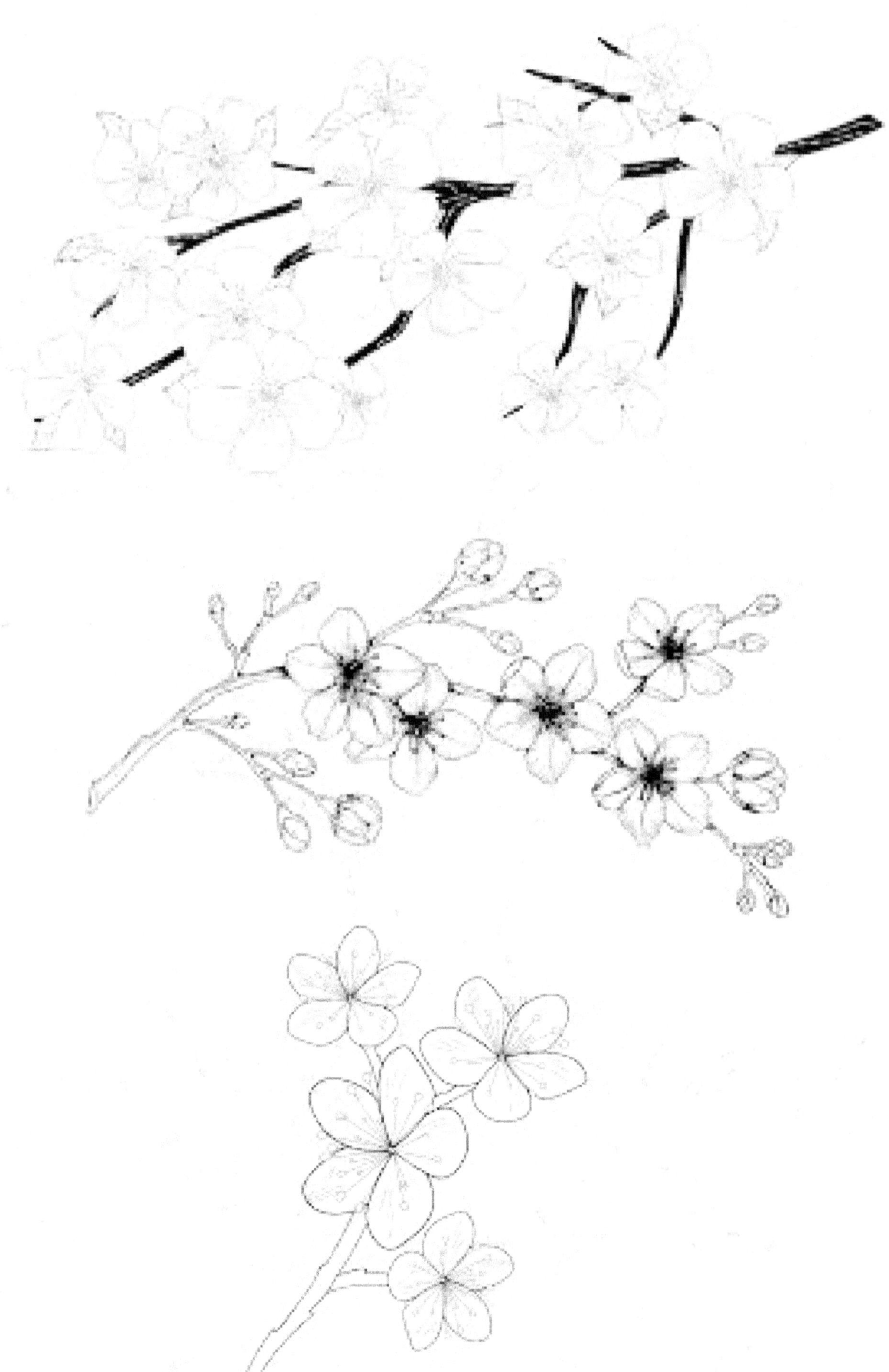

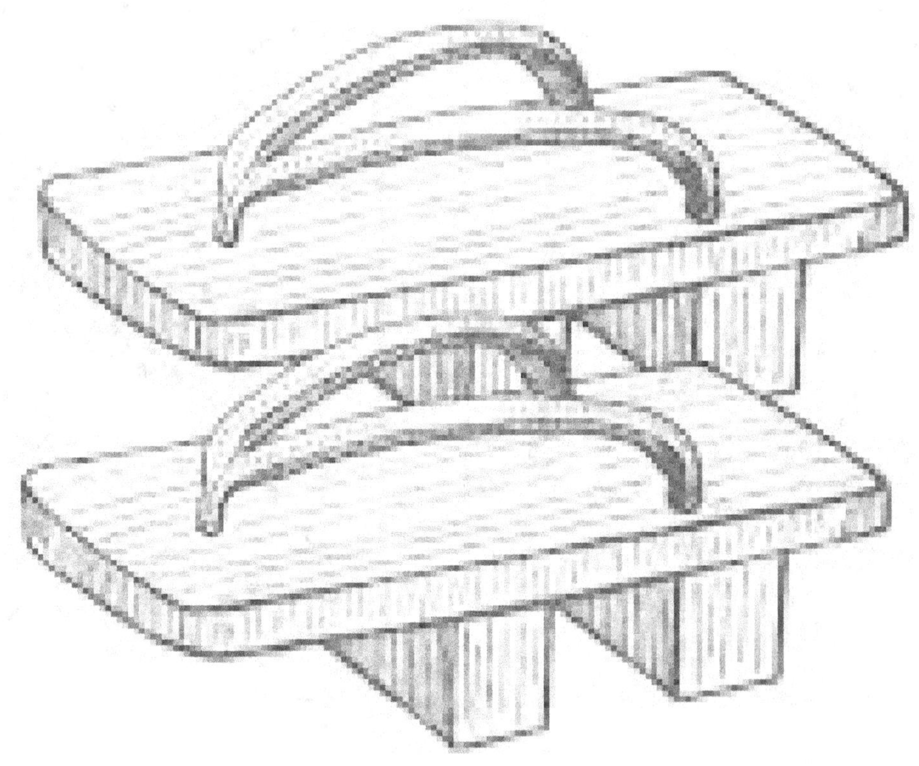

Lirone- Wike

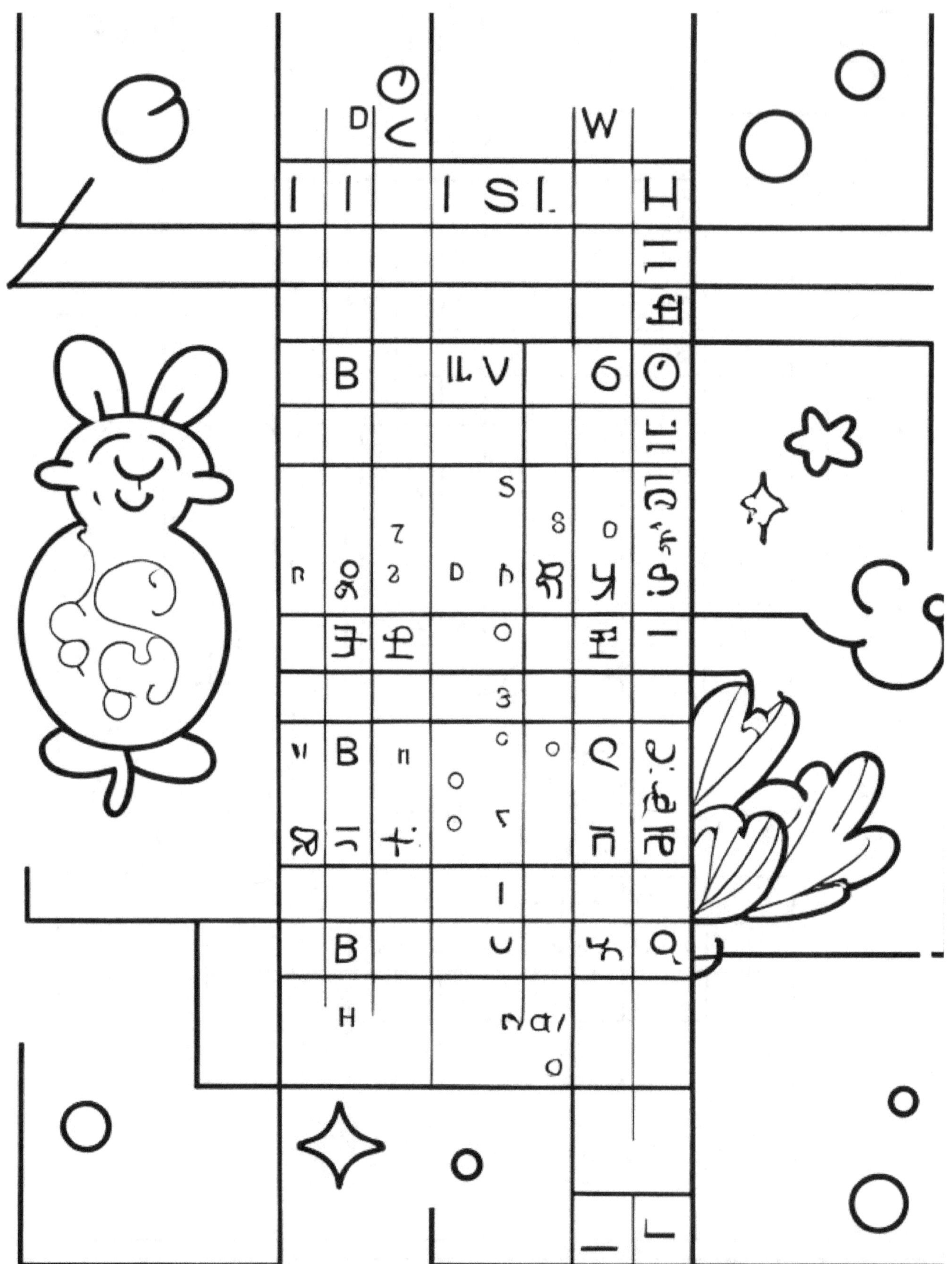

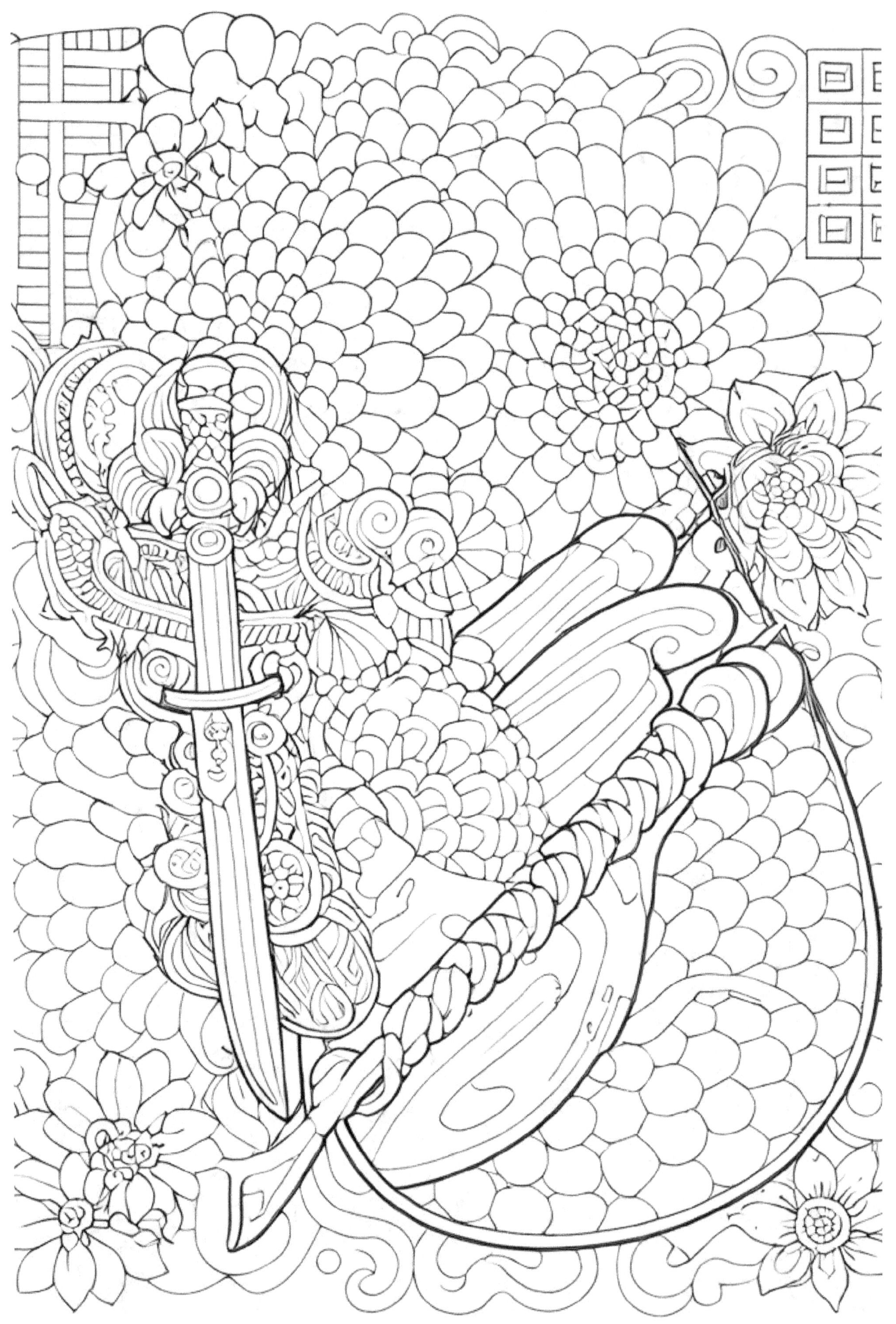

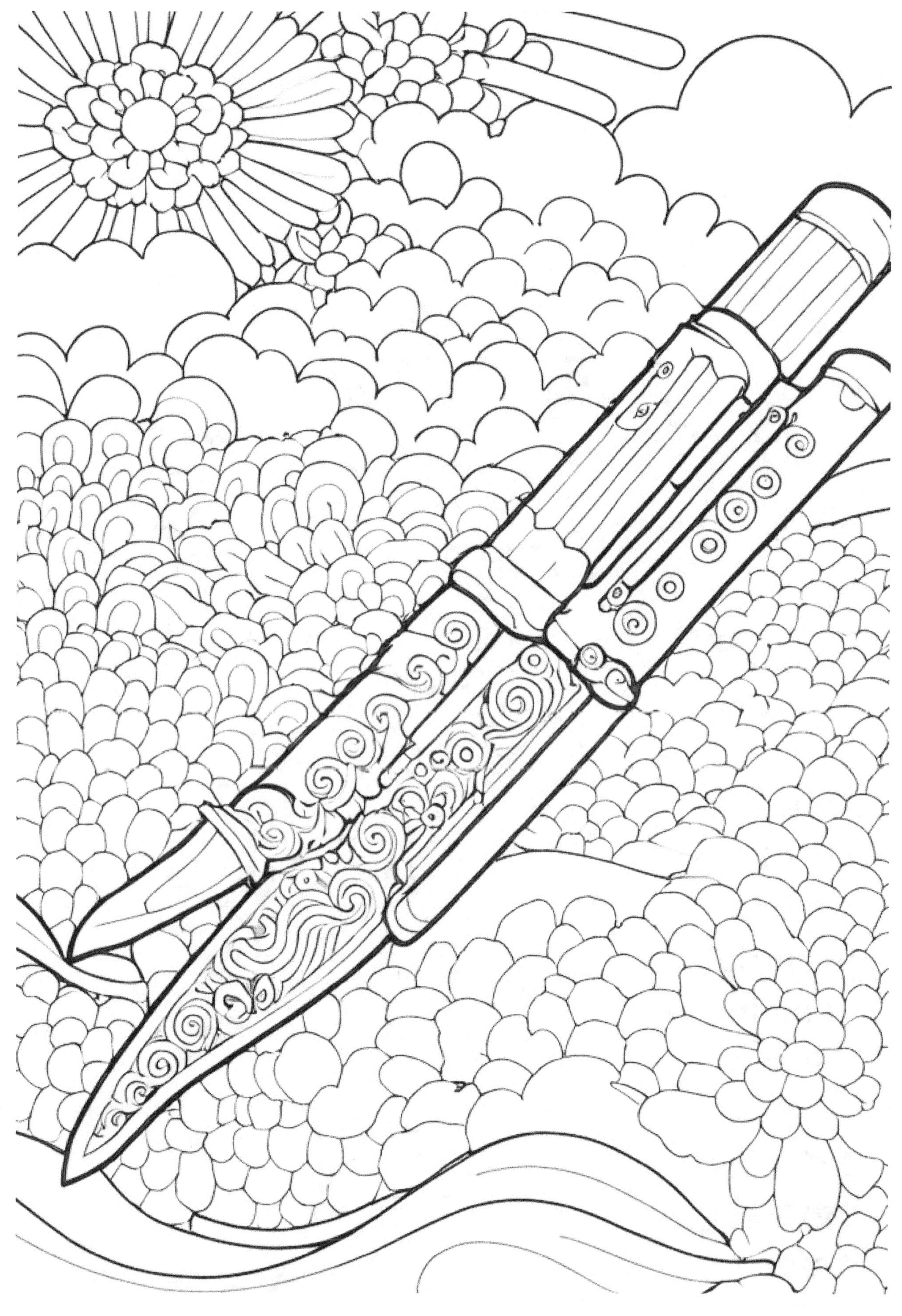

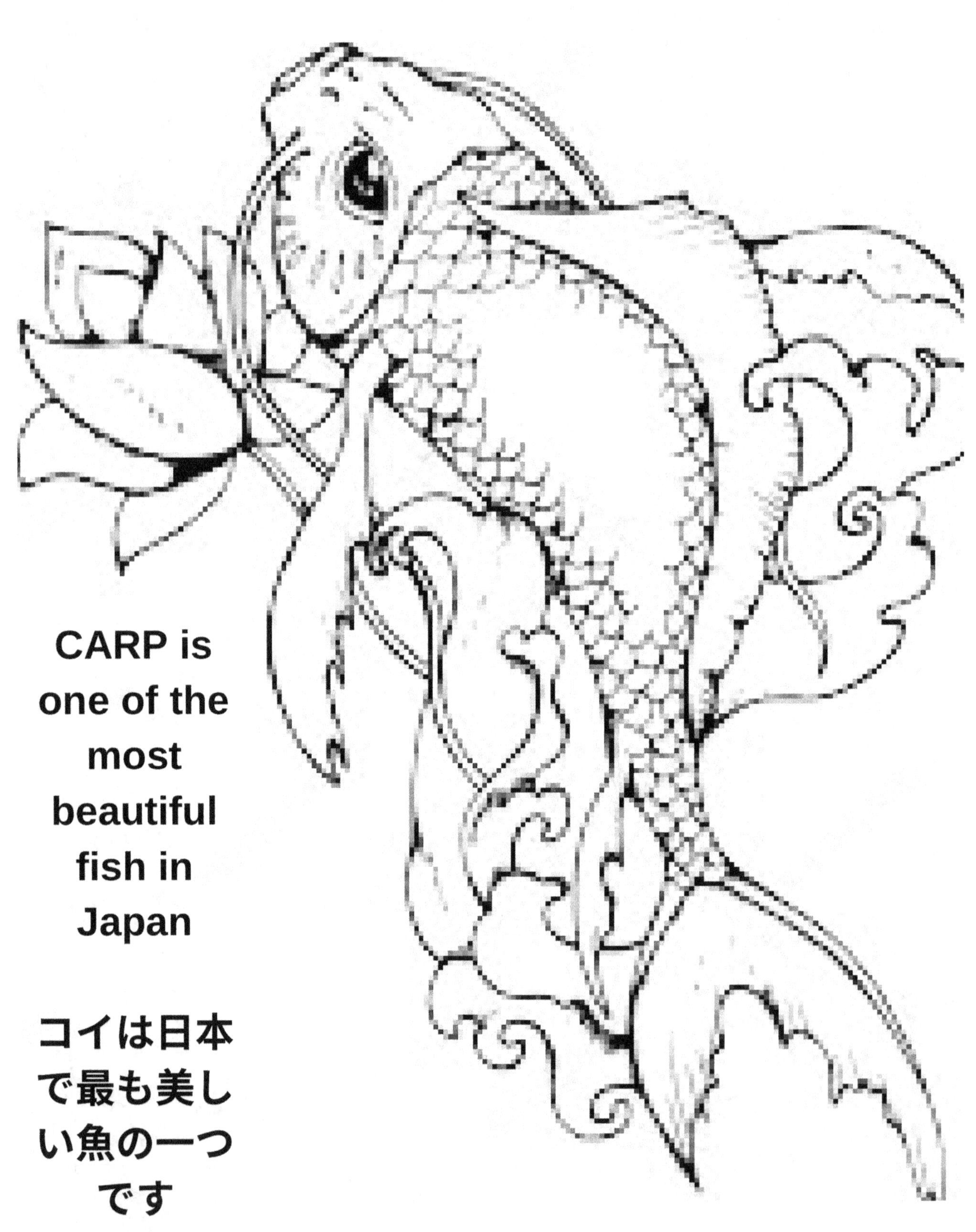

CARP is
one of the
most
beautiful
fish in
Japan

コイは日本
で最も美し
い魚の一つ
です